part of what
makes our life
in Reno so
nice

The Caution of Human Gestures

w/ love -
Ann

... the happiness
is the underlyer ...

The Caution of Human Gestures

Ann Keniston

David Robert Books

Published by David Robert Books
P.O. Box 541106
Cincinnati, OH 45254-1106

Typeset in Aldine by WordTech Communications LLC, Cincinnati, OH

ISBN: 193233971X
LCCN: 2004108515

Poetry Editor: Kevin Walzer
Business Editor: Lori Jareo

Cover photo: Derveni Krater (detail of Dionysos and Ariadne), Archeological Museum of Thessaloniki. Reprinted by permission.

Author photo: Theresa Danna-Douglas

Visit us on the web at www.davidrobertbooks.com

Weren't you astonished by the caution of human gestures
on Attic gravestones? Wasn't love and departure
placed so gently on our shoulders that it seemed to be made
of a different substance than in our world? Remember the hands,
how weightlessly they rest, though there is power in the torsos.

—Rilke
Trans. Stephen Mitchell

Acknowledgments

Grateful acknowledgment is made to the editors of the following journals, in which some of these poems have appeared previously, sometimes in different versions:

The Antioch Review: "Matter and Spirit"
Carolina Quarterly: "Marker"
Crazyhorse: "In a dream, two years after" and "Persephone Awake"
descant: "Residue"
Green Mountains Review: "The Intruder" and "The Sheen"
Interim: "Bridge," "Rupture," and "Zero"
The Kenyon Review: "1961" and "Our Alliance"
The Laurel Review: "Full Moon"
The Madison Review: "The Turning Away"
Michigan Quarterly Review: "The Request"
Mystic River Review: "Deflection"
North American Review: "Booze" and "Poem"
Pequod: "Persephone in Autumn"
Poet Lore: "The Suitcases"
Red Rock Review: "A Lesson"
River City: "What's been hidden in the dark"
River Styx: "Bric-a-brac," "The Gesture," "Old Grief," and "Stigmata"
Salamander: "Another Journey"
Shade: "Anniversary," "Second Language," and "Simile"
Southern Poetry Review: "Burial"
Spoon River Poetry Review: "The Fat Boy"
Tampa Review: "Two Laws"

"The Yielding" originally appeared in the *Grolier Poetry Prize Annual 1996;* "1961" was reprinted in *The Emily Dickinson International Society Bulletin.*

Many thanks to the Blue Mountain Center for the Arts, the Ucross Foundation, the Virginia Center for the Creative Arts, and the Ragdale Foundation for providing the time and space in which many of these poems were written, and to the Somerville (MA) Arts Council, the Sierra Arts Foundation, and the Nevada Arts Council for grants supporting the manuscript's completion.

I am grateful to the teachers who supported my writing, including Richard Strier, Sharon Olds, and Gail Mazur. Martha Serpas and Meg Tyler helped with the manuscript at several crucial moments. And to Julia Lisella and Cammy Thomas, who patiently, generously, and rigorously read nearly all these poems and offered steadfast and loving support to their author, special thanks.

For Eric

Contents

One

And then the material world called me back with its awful
specificity of smell, color, taste and I nearly forgot
the realm of the spirit, in which suffering is pure.
In the frescoes of Giotto, the visible nearly obstructs
transcendence and replaces it with ordinary
human pain, so when Jesus finally conquers it,
and rises, in stiff drapery, his feet scarcely point, as if
he were still constrained by the earth, or
expected gravity's triumph at any moment
over upward motion. And so I longed again
for the particular circumstances in which
I first was harmed: the tiny lilies of the valley pressing
the house foundation with their overpowering
odor, the pool where orange fish lived, rising
halfway to the top so the water shimmered,
and the parental bedroom, two figures
under the covers waiting for my touch to release them
into motion. How much simpler to relinquish
my responsibility and leave them furled,
to choose renunciation, in which pain
still throbs, but powerlessly, like cloth so thin you see
right through it. Wouldn't anyone prefer to dwell
beyond the last outpost of the represented world,
where the perfect triangle, circle, square are suspended
from the pulsing whiteness that is all there is there?
Even then, eyes pressed shut against
whatever landscape I was trying to deny,
I was talking to myself, which is how I venerate
the trivial, half recovered, half imagined world.

I started to starve in September's
first weeks, and by the time
I descended to earth, I was so small
I caused my mother scarcely

any physical pain, my body
slipping out of hers the way a coin
vanishes through a pocket's seam
and becomes invisible, except

I was made visible, and lay
in the clear small cage around which
doctors hovered, trying to determine
whether I was damaged, or how, and my mother

vowed never to reveal to me this first
way she'd failed me, and all that fall,
the heavy new volumes
of Dickinson's *Complete Poems* were piled

onto bookstore shelves in every city
in America, and lay there
silently, a cushion of empty space
surrounding each poem, until a reader lifted one

and, holding open the book in some cramped
public corner, read for the first time
"My life closed twice,"
"My Life had stood—a Loaded Gun—"

But I must venerate it too,
how it takes so many forms
like a god, who makes his body
impermanent so as to take
pleasure more easily, as Zeus
became lithe, almost feminine,
to tempt and then coerce
the maiden who he knew
beforehand swooned
at the touch of feathers
giving way to swansdown,
and after he had had her,
he invented another bodily disguise.
I've seen it wait, half visible,
sometimes for months, for years,
until every alternative has failed.
In this, as everything it touches,
its intelligence is unblemished by
deceit, since the transparent
glassful, like a glass of water,
elixir of life, or an empty glass
is incapable of distortion but merely
forces the acknowledgment
of what has till then
been unarticulated. How delicately
it alternates compassion
with ferocity, never collapsing
the way a daughter might
but inspiring, like an accomplished lover,
however brutal, a kind of awe.
And how reverently it touches

the foulest places, and lodges itself
there, progressing so slowly
she scarcely notices she's lost
first appetite, then thirst
for water, that she's become
accident-prone, so
when at last she sees
her obligation to
what it's made of her,
she feels unloosed, released.

My sister and I must have loved each other,
at least, when our mother found the two of us
equally to blame, equally innocent
and therefore ceased to distinguish us.
I think it happened the night we told her
our father was remarrying and
she broke a glass on the ceiling
and called our father up to list the ways
he'd hurt her while we witnessed it.
Or we were upstairs in my sister's bed
or mine and heard only a few
words of her conversation with him, or maybe
she whispered into the phone and we heard
only hissing. We must have been afraid of her,
but at least we were *us*, my sister and I
two copies of the same girl, for once
not rivals, not liars. All those years
we kept devising new ways to hurt each other, except
for the few times we hardly remember because
they were the worst times, when
we shared something, although
it was only pain, like lifting a heavy suitcase,
each of us supporting a little less than its full weight.

The Fat Boy

He stumbles down the steps of middle school
so awkwardly, I have to hate him.
My girlfriend started this; she's thin as a stick
but her initials are the same as his.
I'm eager to find someone to despise.
At home, no one recognizes
what's happening to me.
My nipples itch, my parents are so busy
fighting I'm afraid to interrupt. Safe
in our giggling intimacy, Christina and I
call Chris "greaseball" until I half believe
his skin is oily as cooked meat
or a softened butter stick.
We're smart, tall, and came in fourth
and third on Field Day just two years ago.
Sometimes we talk about sticking a pin in him
to shrink him into a normal boy. "Grease
would flood the halls." I know
Christina's secrets; she knows
something in my family's about to give.
Six months from now, with half my family I'll move
to another city and be the new kid, loitering
for months around the fringes. For now we're
like skinny birds hovering around their
incidental victim, our catastrophes
folded tight inside us, safe—
like a substance under pressure, concealed
until it's spilled.

The summer we knew
our family would never again
be whole, our bodies—my mother's,

my sister's and mine—spun
every night over the beach,
performing, with each

lifted arm and leg, our sundering.
That was how we found
the residue, like salt

stuck to our bodies or
what's left over after everything
has been divided

or a translucent rock shard exposing
its origin—the shells
around which it formed

a hundred million years ago,
whorled, perfect reminders
of what's inaccessible. The bare

black line of sand
on which we balanced
and the water beside it

murkily repeating
the moon's glitter
contained, we imagined,

what had not been
harmed or lost or given away,
a shimmering version

of our dearest possessions
we moved among though
they remained lost,

and then, the last night
of August, we saw we'd accrued
a heap of debts, which we

had to start paying then
and keep paying
until we were nearly destitute.

I kept being drawn to images of emptiness.
Or synonyms for "futility." I had a kind of collection,
which meant I must have wanted something after all.
Or that was the struggle.

                     I was thinking about a particular morning
in bed. It was one month exactly since our anniversary.
Then I remembered eating the soft, sweet cheese
wrapped in pastry hidden in our salad, the two of us dressed up
for each other, a celebration we tried all evening
not to ruin. My thesaurus of lack, my pile of consolations
for what we failed to make, or had made, then
couldn't keep—I'd devoted myself to trying to transform
that absence, until at last I saw it was too pure.
And then history remade itself in the image of loss,
and love fell away and left a gash.
What could I do but touch it, since
the doubters were restored to faith that way. No—
not even a gash, just a place where nothing was, where
a building's been knocked down, then cleared away.
Where nothing was, but it was like nothing else.

Old Grief

The night we watched the comet's blur
beneath the moon's curled tip, we were bickering again
beside the windy lake. There must be some need in us
for exactly this kind of unhappiness. Or we're
its passive medium, like air dumbly transmitting
waves of light. I can't recall why the grappling began
in the story of Jacob, whether the angel
demanded to be wrestled or Jacob, bereft, far from home,
ached to touch the man who waited patiently near him
without recognizing his adversary as God's ambassador.
Standing cheek to cheek, elbow to elbow,
staring in the same direction, how can we endure
the mystery of our separateness? Or let
our old grief illuminate what we can't see, as the moon
is made visible by the sun's absence. Remember our disappointment
staring up at what was immobile and small? Like reaching into love
and realizing it's constructed of a hundred shards
temporarily pressed together. Or touching the hand
that should have grasped yours strongly and realizing
it's too weak to vanquish.

The Yielding

Last summer, when we camped in the high
cold fields below Mount Rainier, we couldn't stop

touching the old sadness, which began in him
but I took it from him as if it were palpable,

a breakable burden someone had to tend,
until I possessed it and he was freed

and could comfort me. I don't want to remember
tenderly our awkward shifting toward each other

in our sleeping bags, his hands on my cheeks
and hair, inviting me to give up everything

that kept me from him, because it harms me
to believe, as I must believe, because I keep

repeating the same series of gestures over and over,
that *to yield* is *to love*. Afterward we lay

side by side in the black prickly grass, watching
for meteors which had probably been falling around our tent

that whole time, although it was nearly too late
for them, patiently, exhaling when one streaked through

the periphery of our vision, and the next day,
the meadows of bright blue and yellow wildflowers

we hiked up through nearly obliterated
what we wanted to forget. At the wild

opening out of space near one of the lesser peaks,
from which the whole mountain was visible, we must

have believed for a moment that what hobbles us
might also restore us though we should know

by now it keeps us in thrall, that our completely
dark bodies curving around the entity

we've been shielding for years might help us locate
and enter its apparent opposite, the expanse of light

without center or edge we came to at last,
and sat in, bathing our swollen feet in mountain water.

Like a thing that wants to yield, and having
laid itself down and become infinitesimal,
ceases to matter. Like the dress in the novel,
pale green silk, that she bent over, mending,
while he could not utter the words and so
nattered on. And then the sky, the
blot of cloud like an enormous fuzzy garment laid out
over the Sierra. All these years inside the compulsion
to hurt, be hurt or have been hurt, I couldn't
trace the hurt. Or traced it without any fear.
Like my childhood misperception
about sex: that it was necessary but
uncomfortable. If I could discard it and inhabit
the discarded part for a while
and thereby be freed. Or chink off
not the "hurt" but the memory of it
dislocated after years working to turn it into
a hamster or kitten tame enough to be
lifted back into its rightful place. If it
could trust me. Or I could find the simile
by which division could be not healed
but made to shimmer. Or lay down
everything except the effort to love.
And having given all that up, to be
not empty but still, a row of garments
on their hangers or a landscape occupied
nearly wholly by sky, just a few inches
of sand or dirt at the canvas bottom.

What's been hidden in the dark,

the skin having discerned
its underlayer: this thing caught there,
not just there but released by the lips
from any patch of shoulder or neck or chest:
like loosening the cords
so the prisoner can wiggle his extremities, no, like
after swimming when you lie down on the towel
and the sky and trees spin: our near-vertigo at this expanse
of each other, which lets us reenter whatever
we've forgotten like avoiding in the dark
a piece of furniture that's long since been removed:
as if all we could do was spread thinly the dense
overlay onto ourselves or strip off
what's inessential with our chafing palms
until it falls away in sheets at which
we would marvel if we could see them
like tree bark hidden in the long grass
all around the tree, or dilute with our tongues
the firm solid wafer of body, pressing at that alien
boundary until it softens, then melts,
or thrust at it so hard we feel the altitude shift in our ears,
like bursting out of the water and wondering
at how loud the world has grown
until what has been inaccessible
becomes the thing without which
we cannot endure, the knot around which
the intricate construction splays out,
balance point for that improbable teetering pose

Two

Look how Narcissus perished, so still

so patient before that illusion
                    not of perfection but perfect
ardor, the black-gray lips quivering,
each lash distinct and tremulous.
                    Who wouldn't wait
in suspense before the
                    one-in-a-hundred, -in-a-thousand
chance of response?
                    And above him, all the little stars
hung on invisible threads. And the planets,
caught between certainty of form and of motion,
advanced, majestic and
                    elliptical.

And at the center of my yearning: what? The brokenness
had become nearly solid, like a shadow or
                    God, invisible
but everywhere manifest if you know how to look.
And when I touched whatever-it-was, far from
vanishing, it burgeoned or jangled against the thing
adjacent, anterior or
                    beneath so there was a kind of music or
a screeching sometimes which confirmed that he'd robbed me
not on purpose but through mere
                    inattention, which
is how I transformed him into someone I had no choice
but to love.
                    How patiently I wavered before the shimmer of

that absence, conjuring, perfecting its dimensions
until I couldn't *not* see: oh but with

                                  such tenderness, my fingers even now
grazing the edges of what I'm not done forsaking.

At Salpêtrière, the hysterics
enacted their symptoms—
babbling, limping, swooning—at fixed hours

before a roomful of curiosity-seekers,
until Freud, lurking around that theater,
prised open their bodies

and read from them till every refusal
signified a ravenousness
for eros. For a moment

after the home pregnancy test's
three minutes had elapsed, I misread
the single blue line surrounded

by a white expanse—negative—
for confirmation. It took less than a second
after I'd turned, not away from desire

but into it, for my *Yes*
to reverse itself, as if
in the overheated bathroom

an exotic, delicate flower had suddenly
bloomed, then collapsed before
what was, the way Robert Lowell's

late revisions, a series
of pencilled *No*'s, *Never*'s, *Un*'s
above the neutral typeface,

hardly altered the poems' original meaning,
although they may have
allowed him, indirectly,

through a kind of subterfuge,
to articulate what all along
he'd wanted to say.

We saw for a minute
what our half-cells joined to make
in sterile dishes outside our bodies,

enlarged, projected
on the TV monitor just above
my raised, spread thighs:

three balls of cells. So life begins
in emptiness and light: these few
stuck-together soap bubbles like

the tetrahedrons we drew in chemistry class,
in which atoms were
identical circles pressed together, or

that was how we represented
the idea of them. The screen
darkened, someone took my hand,

the doctor put our three embryos into
a catheter, then into me, and we marveled,
which meant we began

to mourn, since they were
released from every
natural confine and so

inaccurate approximations of what
no one, not even we, could
locate, measure, make endure.

Stigmata

Twenty-four months of attempting to invoke
a third body, ghost
daughter, figurine thin enough to slide easily out
from where our bodies joined:
we were worshiping failure
every time we lay down on the bed's white slab
and pulled off our clothes
and waited to be sundered. By then
every neutral thing spun around our desire—
pale peelings on the floor
or the moon in first quarter, tenderly supporting
its absent body inside that narrow
arc of reflected light. The girl in New York State,
when her palms began to bleed in church, had recently
ceased menstruating. I loved that part of the story, as if
receiving the stigmata were like giving birth except
inadvertent and without issue. And how practical
the miraculous seemed, effortlessly recycling
the materials of bodily shame into transcendence.
Experts never knew whether she'd hoaxed it,
or was held too tightly by some illness ever to be cured.
What could we do but kneel before the few
fragmentary signs of divinity, which can be touched
but not interpreted, the body helplessly, jubilantly
abandoning its humanity until it is
a trembling string waiting to be plucked again,
an empty, burnished cup.

Marker

To find a marker for the invisible losses,
what never had a body, not even
botched, malformed, wounded fish—

drops of wine on a dinner plate, running
together, or a row of pebbles on the sill
or in the garden, specks of quartz
too deep in grass to see—

or to wear a secret talisman marking
what we do not have, so we can
recognize one another . . .

I can only imagine
how our embrace wouldn't be:
outside the realm of weeping,
the awkwardly expressed
pity of others, the longing that partly
consoled us until failure
prohibited it—

She stands among us like a plant
that blooms all winter, unnatural.
Her presence soothes us, tells
what we are not. We are not thin-

stalked children walking the windy field.
We never crawled up her ten flights
on our knees. We hold ourselves tight
against us. No one really believes

the dead stay with us, or even in us.
There's nothing to dream of but funerals,
the bodies inside their boxes still as dolls.
Mother's body, father's, death a dailiness,

a ritual. The rain could wash away the stone,
dirt, pry open the plastic box that holds her,
what she is now. I'd like to hold her
in my hands, ash, gold, lumps of bone

and let her wash away. I'd recount
everything that happened since she died, not
with my mouth, but touching that
heap of dust. I'd put her in my mouth

because I miss her and I don't know how to talk.
Tongue on tongue, tooth on tooth,
I'd rub my life against her death
and be cured, or fall asleep, or wake.

—for RCK

In a dream, two years after

her death, she returns to walk with me
beside the unused tracks. She's speaking
in the voice I have granted her, the voice I want to hear.
She doesn't recognize the buildings on either side of us.
They are abandoned, thin-walled, with boarded windows,
but she thinks they are apartments. She's forgotten
about detention, deportation, genocide,
she's innocent of all forms of suffering because
she is dead, she has already traveled back
to her mother's country, carrying her mother's fine-
woven linen handkerchief for comfort. Because she was
a victim, and died in her car alone with no one to hold her head
when she set it down on the steering wheel to rest it
and it filled with blood that last
hour of her life, no one to say *love* or *solace*,
she is offering me, I am offering myself
in dreaming this another chance. So I let myself
dream an accident, and avert it, shout *stop*,
leap from the car and scoop up the infant she nearly
hit, and I save her, this child
who must be her and also me
restored to innocence, solaced. I save her, I'm
saved by her, and I want to keep on sleeping, even though
I'm dreaming of danger, but the danger
wakes me, and she's lost again to me, the way
she left before I could let my voice, whatever
my voice sounds like, lift from my mouth and speak.

—for RCK

Proximity

Another's lost, his wrecked body freed
from suffering only morphine at the end

reduced, turned into ash. A hokey voice in a dream
or other sign that he's all right, has moved

to the next level of some hierarchy or been
allowed to persist on earth, like the nearly useless

angels in Wenders's *Wings of Desire,* who occasionally
lay a palm on someone's shoulder to unmake

for a moment their suffering: that would be enough,
to imagine him released

from bodilessness, having been granted
any old body like a patched-together

shirt, in which to stand nearby somewhere
and measure his proximity to what

his life never was.

—for RM

And then you're suddenly distracted
by the play of light on the quilt and the pain
without vanishing becomes a thing
misplaced or abandoned on the curb
before you left that old city forever
and then thought better of so you tossed it
into the suitcase but haven't yet
unpacked. It's almost a comfort or
stuck into a realm you can't begin to fathom
without hours of study and a shelf-full
of reference books. Not that it's not inside you
because it's what made you and also
what you've been resisting, like a clingy
friend you'd like to be rid of but you can't
turn away from her particular
awkwardness or self-absorption
not out of loyalty but because
she loves you and knows just how you are.
So you feel as you do after an illness,
groggy, weak, stumbling into the kitchen,
the sun blithely spilling
all over the table, the floor, the glittering cups
someone has begun setting out.

Bric-a-brac

In my favorite joke, Abe calls his buddy Mo from the afterlife
to let him know death isn't so bad, since his routine
has hardly changed—he still spends his time eating, sleeping,
making love. Mo thinks Abe's in heaven,
but he's wrong: Abe's calling from the Midwest
where he's come back as a buffalo. Last night,
listening for an hour to my lover's disembodied voice
repeating the old repertoire, I tried to imagine
what I couldn't see—his lips, his fingers
curled around the receiver—and failed. So the joke
is funny because it's wrong: the body isn't what persists.
All spring when I lay on the special table and let waves
reveal my interior, then gave away another vial of blood,
I was waiting for my body to separate from me,
evade diagnosis and therefore be free—mere muscle,
fluid, bone. Sometimes I want to float
in the cold black lake until stillness radiates from my center.
Or convert the bric-a-brac surrounding failure into
some dividend, as sometimes in the midst of insomnia,
inconsolable, I find I'm in a place I can't get to any other way,
where bright yellow flowers, improbably,
since they have never been cared for, are blooming.

Full Moon

Somewhere above clouds and rain and fog
the moon is blazing, full moon, illuminating
whatever's up there—all the stars, maybe,
the sheen around the earth. Five days of rain,
early spring, mud, the river rising. I'm swollen
with someone else's life, so I'm repeating
the obsolete full moon prayers, prayer of the silver arrow,
prayer to the virgin setting her hand over the eyes of one
rapacious youth, another, another, until the mossy earth
is littered with beautiful sleeping bodies.
And the prayer for the women who rose in a different form
from mud, prayer for the unborn swirling in amnion,
eyes glued shut, clasping and unclasping tiny fingers.
Someone locked me in this room with wall-to-wall,
three lamps, a table, a clock outside
marking every hour, but gently. Or I chose it: this room
rather than twenty identical ones. Someone
is watching me, insomniac, counting hours,
days, weeks, putting the dishes back into their places,
a row of bowls, a row of glasses, spoons, and so on.
Moon of the unseen, moon of suffering wadded up
in every heart, moon of those who died in winter,
and lay in the cold—is this a dirge? a prayer?
Those babies have gone nowhere yet,
poor strangers, without sex, without names,
too tiny to survive anywhere but in the dark.

Three

Every trip I lose another.
Inevitably it contains what I think
is most valuable. Inevitably
there's some catastrophe—a fire,
a deportation, the need to leap
from the train's tiny window.
I know I seem like a silly heroine.
I know this loss, like any loss,
could be interpreted in several ways.
Without my heap of wrinkled clothes,
reams of pages each containing
one or two trivial words, I'm finally
"without baggage," free
from what coerced me
to walk stoop-shouldered, in an attitude
of mourning. Or, the opposite—
in losing what I own, I lose what I am.
What can I do but stumble
like the figure of Loss down the cobbled
streets of foreign cities, rattling
at doors which do not, cannot open.
Or it *is* my fault somehow. I'm unable
to learn from my mistakes, I stubbornly
won't laugh at adversity.
I'm like the obstinate, tragic
cataract patient who, thanks to modern
medicine, sees for the first time the world
in its sharp-edged
simultaneity but is never so happy
as when, in the dark, she sees again
by touching. Sometimes I imagine

finding them, row after row
of suitcases, duffels, attachés
arranged by color and size
in the cavernous station
of some city I haven't been to yet.
I could hardly go down on my knees
before these things I've learned to do
without. I couldn't carry them away,
not half of them.

or another part of the same one, with
the same landscape streaming past the unrolled
windows, cows huddled in the barn's
wedge of shade, and in the distance the blue-green
sea that we aspire to because it is
too cold to enter, and beneath every
hilltop, a city of dead bodies. Everything
we wanted to escape has followed us, even
our insomnia, nights on strange mattresses with
the familiar voice yammering in our ears
in a monotone that soothes us but refuses
to shut up, although we rise each morning
and attain without effort another blue day like requesting
beauty or motion and receiving that wish.
And you, with your slight limp, who resemble me
so much that strangers call across the road,
are you two brother and sister?,
inhaling summer's sweetness while
mist builds at the water's surface and crickets
sing in the goldenrod—you hold
your burden in your arms like an infant as if
weeping would help, to collapse like children
by the side of the road. *At least I am loved*
by someone, at least my body is as known to you
as your own and we're moving from vista point
to vista point, and down into the muck
of low tide that pulls at the soles of our shoes
to observe the clench and release of crab claw, bubbles
rising from little holes, the fronds—

so thin—unfisting, moving in the slight
current until for a moment we turn and marvel at
what used to bind us to the earth.

Bridge

Last night, the dreamed bridge
                    suspended,
glittering, for miles over the chasm or desert over which
cars varoomed, blurs of light marking
                          the narrow lanes
while I sought the exit I'd already missed; impossible
to descend from, rampless
                silver rope in space,
a line of x-ed girders and cables obeying
the laws of physics, extending
against the earth's curve or mirage of it.
When it woke me, did I reach for him
whom I've vowed to love, and have loved
steadfastly and hungrily,
                having imagined an invisible
cord binding us with which we can
                  tug each other
out of danger? I lay alone in my
drench, dim blur outside the windows:
                    easier, still, to yield
to what I know I'm culpable in, as if love were the junk
we'd accrued, insulation, bulky soundproofing jammed
between ourselves and whatever's worse
rather than what might otherwise have permitted us,
having removed volition, appetite, body,
to drift like seeds
           or dust on the airbanks.

Seeds

It's the perfection with which
they're engineered
that amazes, as if
someone knew every effort
would fail, the scant
fibers surrounding each seed
so ready for flight
it's nearly impossible to hold one
between my fingers.
They've gathered
against the wall, gotten stuck
in spiderwebs.
They make the air
visible, drifting sideways like
commas or little birds,
as if the absent and
dead could be punched out
from grief like a set
of paper dolls, with
bodies, even if the wrong ones,
and all this time
I'd been wishing
for the wrong thing.

Unwritten Poems

Sometimes I imagine the events, revelations, secrets
I've wanted for years to write about
but failed to find language for

collapsing effortlessly into poems
somewhere else, their long or short lines,
their stanzas or bulky blocks of text

visible to me though not quite legible, the way
my writer friends occasionally tell anecdotes
so funny and sad, they reveal everything their frail or

tightly bound or unflinchingly serious poems
could be, if only they could trust
such fleeting gracefulness or candor about

the everyday, as if all our failings were less
a matter of talent than of having
a pencil ready at the right moment.

And I like to imagine a reader
so distracted or naïve, she's never heard
the confessional impulse is doomed

in contemporary literature or poetry
must be succinct and precise, who's so eager
to locate her own Loss, History, Happiness

that she lifts the offered sheaf
and admires most what's earnest, filled
with yearning, and flawed.

The Gesture

I was still afraid to touch my father when I thought
he was dying. I only slipped my hand
into his hand before the dangerous
surgery because I couldn't speak, and his wrist was tied
to the bedrail, in proximity to me. I thought
he held it as if he were grateful I was speaking to him
that way, with my body, or maybe
he pitied my awkwardness, but it was only
five or ten minutes until the nurse came in
to tell me to leave, and he was drugged
and in physical pain I couldn't imagine with his eyes
moving separately and his throat so full of phlegm
he couldn't speak, so he couldn't have known
anything new about me then. Afterward,
when he'd come out all right and lay
in a series of rooms convalescing, he reached out his hand
whenever I came in, and waited like a child
for me to take it, like a father
whose relation to his child has not been damaged or
someone who has suffered and in that way
become vulnerable to tenderness, until
he was stronger, and it was no longer necessary.

His First Death

Sometimes it seems beautiful:
the damp raw perfection of my love
shimmering there in his hospital room.
And sometimes a *frisson* at the notion
I could have been left there, the clot
of my resentment dissolved like hair
in a pipe or pumped out.
And how nearly this death approximates
a real one: as if he'd really died and
I were drifting through the streets of heaven,
carrying a wreath or nosegay for him,
something superfluous.

The Intruder

Always, he lays his fingers
on my palm so I'll
insert them into my mouth

to moisten them and gag
and be unable to cry for help.
This is how I engineer

my salvation, just as
after they have forgotten
an atrocity, its victims

return to where it occurred,
and walk past the innocuous
hedges to the bare room

they think they've never seen before
and sit down there. I fashioned him
from whatever materials

were at hand like a scarecrow
or an effigy so I'd never
hesitate to join him. Terror

preserved me, the way every night
just before the ultimate
humiliating act, I waken, restored

to the heap of colorless pillows
on which I recline
like an actress performing

for the hundredth time the end of fear.

Being in love is like being dead.
I lie very still and wait
while the clock spins its hands. Passivity
makes me beautiful. I'm
a vessel for seeds
he feeds me that explode in my mouth.
If I enjoy their lusciousness
I'll be trapped.
If I remove my clothes and move
I'll always be thirsty.

What do I desire? Not spring
when the topheavy flowers sway
on their stems, excessive
blossoms festoon the trees.
Not the reenactment of
the kiss and wail.
When it's time to leave
I'll slither out of here without
once using the clicks and moans
of ordinary speech, I,
who used to mark every occasion.

I'll stand before the muddy field
and watch another morning begin.
I'll start to walk.

Persephone in Autumn

In the season of rotting fruit, when
crickets hiss their last requests
and petals flutter off

the late bloomers, beauty's
final flare-up before the dead months,
I, who despise airports,

endings, whose sentences simply
trail off, feel for a moment regret's
familiar throb, and harbor for a moment

the illusion I can choose among
several appealing options, only one of which
is obedience. No one had to teach me

beauty exists to embody the inevitable.
If I stand in an empty meadow, a golden
expanse that doesn't wave or tremble,

it reveals the terrain in me
that's withered, unredeemable.
If I elect a life of silence

and close my mouth around my tongue
to let it rest, doesn't that demonstrate
I never learned to make a sound?

As if my love of sweetness
proves I know nothing
of bereavement, as if

I've gathered up
all the gold on earth to buy
what only confirms my poverty.

To know everything about   the middle—
being halved or doubled,   teetering at the exact fulcrum,
equals sign of some hardly comprehensible   formulation, so that love
which was where we began   and which remains our obsession
seems sometimes   a mere byproduct of our efforts
to remain upright or collapse when the slippery   sheets rise up
to entangle us,   an envelope into which
we slip and become   invisible, affirming
the old vow to linger just where   the crack was, many-times-
glued-on cup handle, and venerate   not the break or the healing but
how the repair job   can't unmake the bump where the edges don't
quite lap, the finger   retracing that smoothed-over
assurance of rupture until the rift,   having renewed itself, violates
what we thought we'd long since   divided up, then
abandoned, and we find we're still   amateurs, awkward ingenues
who've adopted the poses   of survivors listlessly
contemplating the ruins of their bombed-out city,   clutching our
earthenware bowls,   our strands of beads.

I was trying to love. I was happy, lying in bed
with my boys and whispering.
And always around the edges of my happiness
like a little burned place, the feeling
that love had been yanked out of me
so hard it couldn't be put back.
The love felt like an enactment of love,
not artificial but heightened, like yielding to what
you shouldn't do because of how much
you want it, although you know there will be,
any time now, some retribution.
And when the retribution didn't come, didn't seem
about to come, it was no better.

Four

Poem

It might take as its subject the man I saw last night
in the subway station, grasping a six- or seven-

year-old boy to his chest, then over his shoulder, then
awkwardly in front of him while the ragged-

shirted, dark-faced, long-haired child groaned,
then shrieked without making a human sound. It could recount

the man's steady but infinitesimal progress
toward the turnstile, then out through it, then along

the dim passage to the escalator while from inside
the token booth the fare collector occasionally

interjected in a monotone through her microphone,
"Let the child go," "Let go of his throat," words

the pair of them failed to acknowledge as if they were caught
in some parable of martyrdom from another century

transposed to this half-lit tunnel replete
with passive watchers. Or it could begin with the boy's

patient terrified compulsion to resist
whatever he was being carried out into,

or with we who witnessed and did not intervene,
dropping our tokens in while glancing backward,

watching and afraid to be seen watching in case
the man's wrath might turn on us. And then the poem,

if it's to be worth rereading, must change, and locate
in that scene some incidental or

inherent beauty or through its motion revise
that brutal progress and unmake, too late

of course, ironically, its author's muteness.
Or it should set that observed scene into a context

that partway explains it, affirming through allusion
to the troubled love of sons for fathers,

or the awe or stillness or weakness that links us
the poem as foil to ugliness. I'd rather

keep returning to where I began until I've captured
the delicacy with which that boy raked his nails

along his captor's improbably white forearm,
or consider what impelled me to write this until

it springs open and exposes some secret
about me or my childhood, but the point

is that whatever resting place the poem
arrives at is artificial, though the reader, like

the poet, wants to mark its ending.

Two Laws

Not that pain's
                diminutive or weak but
that it can recede
                and rather than ceasing to hurt
can become part of the background
against which novelty can
                      jangle: not only
this blister or canker just where gum meets inner lip
that yesterday seemed intolerable but now hardly hurts
but how the intensity of self-hatred or fear
dulls to irritation, short temperedness, a tendency
to curse while driving that seem
                              a distraction from
self-hatred or fear.

                And all this time, the other,
counterbalancing scene:
                    how the guilelessness
of those boys has come to seem balletic, though
                          unstaged,

as if they had been created
all at once by some flamboyant, supremely
                            confident god
trustingly inhabiting love's dominion as if
nothing had taught them
to mistrust the ones on whom they are
                        utterly dependent, so that
to care for them is to wait
for injury to lodge itself in them, or for them
                        to set themselves before

Injury, because such perfection
demands this equal,

                        opposite force,
because this law, too, I acceded to when I consented
to their coming forth from me.

The Request

What startles me is the exactitude
with which each of my sister's requests
locates the periphery of what
our father's comfortable with, then pushes
past it so slightly that he grows pensive,
then voices his refusal formally.
And how unswervingly she persists, revealing
no sign of weariness or bitterness, as if
she believed his response
could erase whatever injuries
he once inflicted. Sometimes I think she sees,
or half sees, that she has no choice
but to follow each of his rebuffs
with a new advance, until by now
their nearly simultaneous movements
have become meaningless and gracious,
like the slowed-down gestures
of the men and women practicing tai chi
on the uneven grass of the public park,
whose attempts to extend the same
sequence of thrust and self-shielding
erase, or nearly, their origin in combat.

He seems a delicate,
gawky angel hovering.
Of course he's meant to be
a statue of one—in white,
with wings rising

from the back of his
draped sheet—balancing
on this heap of inverted crates
in the midst of all our hubbub.
The tremor of his lips

and hands reminds us
he's a mortal laborer
who daubed white cream
on face, neck, wrists, and hands,
glued branches to his brow

and whitened them. Yet our wish
is for the illusion he nearly
represents of immortality
conjoined with stillness, so when
a few coins skitter into the pot

and he extends his arms
and smiles with eyes cast downward,
we nearly feel he's granting us
a glimpse into an inner self that's guileless,
though we know we're also meant

to recognize his graciousness
as a ploy to encourage future gifts.
Then he sighs, shifts,
lays fingertips on hips,
and adopts another pose.

And then I think
of you with your
silences, the O's all over
your body I've
plunged myself into or
been afraid to:
how you tilt sometimes
toward me and I prop
something meaningless
beneath or beside you,
like pushing a bit
of rolled-up cardboard
under the leg
of a tilting table or
setting in the place
of nothing a zero,
a gesture that increases
whatever the error was
by a power of ten
and then occasionally
another ten or sometimes
erases it but
impersonally, as if
I had nothing to do
with the hurt or
its abatement.

The Sheen

How small a space injury must occupy,
after all, and how easily
it can be filled with the trivial,

consoling debris of the everyday.
This morning, abandoning
his body, sleep-warm, tasting

of desire's fulfilment, I felt
no violence, not even a surge
of tears reading in the newspaper

of someone's small, heroic act, only
this slight glowing of
everything, the landscapes

from the plane—stilled whitecaps,
the swirl of mountain with its silent
hood of snow—clarified

and cold, which must be
how grief speaks,
mercifully, offering up

the familiar with
this new, nearly imperceptible
hardness, this sheen.

It reasserts itself, sometimes,
from the castings away of dailiness.
And transforms us back into tender creatures
swaying toward each other, groping for tongues, fingers,
sinews. Even after we've returned to ourselves,
and slept, and wakened, and are working again
in the kitchen, it seems like an other thing
that came to us in our bed and impelled us.
And then we see—graciously it lets us
see—that there's no one there but us,
nor has ever been. And this, too, beside
all the other things, we've made.

A Lesson

He won't stop practicing how to crawl:
ridiculous belly-flops, hours rocking back and forth
on elbows and knees without advancing,
then scrambling in the wrong direction as
the desired object recedes. He's already
stoical, as if he sees but can't prevent
the spectacle his string of failures adds up to.
It's why there's pathos in each victory,
his laughter already touched—isn't it?—
with self-knowledge, though he's flushed with joy
at what he's come to through sheer persisting.

Ennuis of French class, trying to distinguish
Quel couleur est le ciel? from
Comment t'appelles-tu? A long-haired
boy is called Michel. We ridicule him

at recess, misinterpreting
again (his silence, the surge
of *something* we feel joining
against him). The recurring

dream years later reversed
our indifference, his shamefacedness:
in a country of indecipherable
street signs (they're in character,

or Greek, or Cyrillic)
we've lost our luggage,
emblem of our bondage
to things. Hardly tragic

but we're frantic, point, outline
in air the missing objects.
The mime's misunderstood. The train
speeds up. Soon it will be time

to wake in terror. And we do,
to find—we've no idea
how we got here—we're fluent, footsore
from standing for so long inside

the room, or field, or house
we always knew had to exist
of shy murmuring in ears, kissed
fingertips accompanied by a phrase

that comes from somewhere...
And to find our intonation
nearly accentless, near-
ly natural, so that the loved one

responds, and comes
at our invitation.

It accomplishes no realignment
                              of light on just-yellow
willow or pavement
                    inflected toward late sun.
And the fugitive sparrows rise up in a clap
and turn and vanish, incising in air
                                      a not-
visible shadow of their passage. Like Cezanne's
black-rimmed peaches: the outline
                                  covered by that orange-pink
overlay, both pure form and
devoid of form. The happiness is
the underlayer. And the porous, blurred surface,
what we pass through, having risen
out of the subway and
                      dispersed.

the gold or bronze relief, or the reproduction
of it I clipped from a magazine,
which I've described in three or four
                        abandoned poems, each
inadequately driving into some whirl
                   of motion,
wordplay, or allusion
            the same scene of devotion
observed or invented two millennia ago.
Its tenderness can't be easily transmuted
into ecstasy—this I've already tried—or even ordinary
happiness, yoked to some gesture
at the breakfast table
            or in the bathroom where
he's showering while I wash at the sink.
How awkwardly the lover's thrown his naked leg
across her thin-clothed one:
              it's unformed,
pudgy, and askew, like the arm he's raised, wrapped
around his head to indicate, it seems,
his ardor. And she, though her gown just grazing nipples
invites his gaze, won't look at him. Nearly
outside history, nearly
            pure, the scene's
touching-funny, like realizing too late the spectacle
you've been puzzling over the allusions in
is a comedy.
       I might as easily have begun
with the landscape I stood before last Sunday,
sore backed and swollen footed, luminous
in the nearly deserted American wing,

                                     haze of light
on water and cliff, against which the actual light,
dimmed through shades,
                        strove; or with my sons'
patter in the car yesterday, eager, incessant, by turns
violent and tender, and how when I turned
to survey their silence, they were hardly visible
inside the highway dark. And if last night, late,
I'd unwrapped
                my arms from his
sleeping chest and risen to write this down

at my desk
            rather than hoping I'd remember
in the morning,
                the poem's early outline
propelling me into sleep, marking
                            my willingness
to sleep,
        the poem would have been
entirely unlike this one,
                        probably, containing some now-
unforeseeable epiphany or leger-de-main, or perhaps
would have retained
                some of this one's shape or
intonation, so that—who knows?—I might
have come to something like
                        this ending point.

Ann Keniston received a B.A. from the University of Chicago, an M.A. in Creative Writing from New York University, and a Ph.D. in English from Boston University. Her poems have been published in *Antioch Review, Kenyon Review, Michigan Quarterly Review, Pequod, Shade,* and many other journals; her essays have appeared in *Gettysburg Review, Threepenny Review,* and elsewhere. Twice a recipient of the Academy of American Poets Prize, she has been a resident at several artists' colonies, including the Ragdale Foundation and the Ucross Foundation, and has received artist's grants from the Somerville (MA) Arts Council and the Sierra Arts Foundation. She is also a scholar of contemporary American poetry, with articles published in *Contemporary Literature* and several anthologies. She teaches English and creative writing at the University of Nevada-Reno and lives in Reno with her husband and two sons.